Our Future Today

Mohammed Dolley Donzo

First Published in 2016
Published by:
FORTE Publications
#12 Ashmun Street
Snapper Hill
Monrovia, Liberia

FORTE Publishing
7202 Tavenner Lane
208 Alexandria
VA, 22306

FORTE Press
76 Sarasit Road
Ban Pong, 70110
Ratchaburi, Thailand

http://fortepublishing.wix.com/fppp

This book or any portion thereof may not be reproduced or used in any manner whatsoever without the expressed written permission of the publisher except for the use of brief quotations in a book review.

Printed in the United States of America.

Copyright © 2016 MOHAMMED DOLLEY DONZO

All rights reserved.

ISBN: 0994630875
ISBN-13: 9780994630872

DEDICATION

To the best Mother in the world,
on whose labor I am who I am
on whose support I can proudly
attribute my educational sojourn
on whose advice I published
Dear Mama, my entire world
Is forever to owed to you

To my Kakon Donzo on whom
my everything leans on.

To all the Ebola Victims whose tragic deaths
Africa is yet to grapple with. May your souls
rest in perfect peace.

To the children of Africa and the world whose
future this generation must work to improve.

Acknowledgement

The compilation of "Our Future Today" was driven by passion. Never would I have written a poem had it not been by God`s grace. My mom is my bedrock and means everything to me. Her hard work and persistence have landed me thus far. Grateful I am for everything mom, Kakon Donzo. To grandfather Alhaj Sedekie Donzo, thank you for being the best grandfather in the world. Thank you for all your support my mentor Saliho Donzo.

Thank You Mr. Stephen Fondia and Mr. Nvasekie Konneh for your editorial support during the first draft of this manuscript. To Mr. D. Othniel Forte, thank you for making this publication possible. Without you, I doubt *Our FutureToday* would have been published by now.

To sisters Amy, Amie, Zainab, Aicha, Mama, Mawa, Manakababay, Malofo and the rest, thank you all for the amazing support. To my uncles Kalifala - KD, Lassana- Dr. J, Lassana –Bobb Bendumadee- Zebo, Abdullai -V. Wire, Fonsia – Chief, Fonsia – Zeco, Methus, KK etc. and Aunty Mayaphine and Mama, thank you all for the motivation and support. To my brothers Morry, Karlu, and Ansu, you have raised the bar for me and made me dream bigger because of your accomplishments.

To Sedeki Kamara, Alieu Nyei, Ahmed Konneh, Morris Kromah, Musa Willie, Richard Donald etc. and Team MONSU, thank you for the supports. To Wifey Haja and Mawa and the kids, love you all.

It's impossible to mention all of those who contributed to making me, and the publication of this book a success. Hence, to those unmentioned, thank you so much for being the unsung protagonists whose contributions have made my dream a reality.

Table of Content

Contents

DEDICATION iii
Acknowledgement vi
Table of Content ix
Poems about humanity, family, Africa & love xii
Have Liberians forgotten so soon where we came from? 1
The World's Problems Are Mine 4
Letter to Nelson Mandela 5
Nothing Is Impossible 6
Women Are Precious Jewels 7
Say No To Human Rights Violations 8
Gratitude 9
The Sea 10
The Clouds 11
Violence 12
Honesty 13
Our Sisters, Our Future 16
A Newly Wedded Sister 17
Forgiveness 18
Grandfather of Grandfathers 20
Family Is Precious 23
Unity in Diversity 24
Our Future Today 26
She Is Special To Me 28
Passion 29
Underestimation 30
From a Child to an Adult 32
You are a Damn Racist 33
The World Must Wake Up 34

Sleep Oh! Sleep	36
Book of Poetry	37
The Rain	38
The Sky	39
They say, We ask	40
Why Denounced Your Culture?	42
I smell World War III	44
Liberia Never Bows Down	45
Poverty	46
Friends	47
Family is Everything	48
My Mother, My Best Friend	49
Priceless Gift	50
Replica of the Devil`s home	52
We have heard about their coming	53
My High School Secret Admirer	54
Motivation	56
First Love Experience	57
My Africa, Your Africa, Our Africa	58
We are tired with you Mr. President	60
Liberia`s Future	62
Bye Bye Ebola	64
Rest in Peace Big Dad Ansumana	66
Africa Needs You Back	67
Soweto Oh! Soweto	68
How dey you	70
ABOUT THE AUTHOR	74

Poems about humanity, family, Africa & love

Have Liberians forgotten so soon where we came from?

Have Liberians forgotten so soon where we came from?
From our inception, degradation of
Native Liberians was the song sang
A song of wound to the native majority
Yet paradise to the settler minority
A song that flogged the Yakpawolos, Nvasekies and Mamusus

Have Liberians forgotten so soon where we came from?
Like a movie watcher, so the natives were ignored
An ignoring they refused to concur with
Whether the 1979 rice demonstration
Unveiled the impatience of the natives;
The message signified political transition

Have Liberians forgotten so soon where we came from?
When the unwelcoming rice demonstration message
Ushered in the 1980 coup
It took native Liberians to the mansion
It gave native Liberians hope for a better future
Yet many "Habitual Thomases" waited for its realization

Only time was the best judge
A court-less judge whose verdict pointed to some progress
Yet an era of tribalism and habitual vices of past mansions

Have Liberians forgotten so soon where we came from?
Whether citizens dissatisfaction ushered the first native regime
The ousting process was bloody and devastating
Like an ocean, so did the blood of thousands flow
Like sheep, so was the first native mansion butchered

Have Liberians forgotten so soon where we came from?
The ousting of the first native regime ushered another political era
An era that polarized the slogan:
"You kill my ma and pa, I will vote for you"
Time was fast to see the repetition of vices
That dominated the regime of the immediate past mansion
Vices that were repeated with high degrees

It was only a matter of time when
The ousting process brought Liberia on its knees
An ousting process that saw blood flowing like water
With no choice, so the leader was forced to bid farewell
A farewell that led to a peace accord
A peace accord that ushered a new political era
Giving peace a chance in a despair nation

Have Liberians forgotten so soon where we came from?
Have we not learned from the 14 years of bloody civil unrest?
Why do we repeat actions that history has taught us lessons from?
Why have we not reconciled and move on as one people?
Like a meteorologist, so the future of Liberia is up to Liberians

Note: This is a free verse poem
11/2011
Monrovia, Liberia

The World's Problems Are Mine

The world`s problems are ours
As long as we keep breathing

It doesn`t have to be our child
Denied education,
Before it becomes our problem
It doesn`t have to be our continent
Threatened by climate change,
Before it becomes our concern
It doesn`t have to be our family
Suffering from a disease,
Before it becomes our worry

The world's too small to neglect each other
Evidence by recent Ebola Outbreaks
Chances will increase for positive results
With sincere actions
The less politicize our response to issues is
The more we create a better place to live

The world`s problems are our problems
Endeavor we all should
To make the world a less fearful place
For the next generation

08/14/Monrovia, Liberia

Letter to Nelson Mandela

Dear papa Madiba,
It's barely a while you left us
Answering the Creator's call
But Papa, already your children forget
To uphold the principles you lived by

You struggled for equality and yet,
They are killing other Africans
You fought for dignity and justice, but
They steal and loot, rape and murder
To justify their economic hardship

So soon they have forgotten
Those that once stood in
Solidarity with them when in need
Oh so soon they ignore those
Fought their battles with them
When others fled conveniently

Dear papa Madiba, once more,
Your children need to hear your voice
You need to tell them to stop
If only we could have you for a day
What should we do now Papa?
We await your respond Papa?
What should we do now?

4/15/Monrovia, Liberia

Nothing Is Impossible

When we need something
Fiercely we should go for it
This oft requires sleepless nights
And countless obstacles
Yet, we must meet the challenges;
By believing that
Nothing is impossible

When we need something
Work we should towards achieving it
By concentrating on the goal
While everything else waits

When we need something
Give up we should never,
For the 'give up' moments
Will visit us countlessly

When we need something
Consider it ours we should
Grab it; claim it
Is all that should be
On our minds

**05/14,
Monrovia, Liberia**

Women Are Precious Jewels

A woman birthed each of us all
Yet some make them sex workers

Women catered to us
Women cared for us,
Women looked after us
Women nurtured us
Women taught us
They are precious
Why make one a sex slave?

We often marry them
We sometimes give birth to one
We at other times are siblings
Why would we even consider
Ill-treating or harming them?

I will end up marrying a woman
Why will I make one a sex slave?
Lean on them we often do
Women should be our most
Precious jewels and not some

Abuse object
A sex symbol
Or a furniture

04/15 /Monrovia, Liberia

Say No To Human Rights Violations

Our songs of freedom are on the way
to those who have forgotten that
there exists, defenders of human rights;
To those who must safeguard
The human rights of our comrades; and
To those at the peak of power

Our letters and signatures are on the way
For we will not stop sending them
Until human rights is a must for all
Our Notes will never get dry
Until no one is detain or manhandle
For speaking truth to power or
For exercising their basic human rights

Our "Write for Rights Campaign" won't stop
Until everyone is a defender of rights;
Until power is not a tool for oppression
Abuse or violation of those basic rights
Until there is no prisoner of conscience
Unfairly held captive, wherever we live

Let`s keep the fire blazing
Let`s keep mounting the pressure
Let`s keep the fight alive

12/14/
Monrovia, Liberia

Gratitude

Gratitude,
our way of saying thank you
To those who are kind to us
Gratitude,
the thing that we give people
when they've done good for us
Gratitude,
the thing that can move
People to do more good
Gratitude,
the thing that is needed by
Everybody at a point in our lives

Like a ladder, so is gratitude
It creates bigger opportunities
Grateful we must be
for everything we have
For gratitude often take us forward
It takes us a step closer to our dreams

07/14
Monrovia, Liberia

The Sea

Sitting at the beach
Looking out quietly
at the sea
Looking at
the rising and falling tides
Feeling the sea's breeze
As nature goes
to and fro; this and that way
Wow! I marvel

As the sea rushes angrily ashore
Then recede calmly back to base
I can't but wonder at nature's beauty
And sometimes, it compels me to ponder
The marvel of creation and the creator

03/14
Monrovia, Liberia

The Clouds

The clouds change colors
The clouds get dark
The clouds let us know
when it's about to rain
when it's just mid-day and
it seems like midnight already
The looks of the clouds at times,
take me back to my childhood days
When we sang in our local dialect:

"Rain! Rain! Come down! Potel! Potel! Go up!"
"Rain! Rain! Come down! Potel! Potel! Go up!"

This popular childhood song
when dark clouds plastered the sky
is what these clouds remind me of today

05/14
Monrovia, Liberia

Violence

The worst solution
to a problem is violence
It narrows the way one thinks.
With thoughts vaguer,

Options limited

Limited options often
produce bad ones

It only seeks to destroy
It never tries to build
Even those times it seems
an option, it is in truth an
emotional decision that
one often regrets later

Honesty

Honesty, often is difficult
Some fail others succeed
Key ingredient it is
To character,

Honesty is the key
To leading an exemplary life
One worthy of chance
Worthy of inspiring humanity
Worthy of building an air castle

**08/14
Monrovia, Liberia**

Words

Words I have used
to educate
to persuade
to motivate people
Words I have used
to disagree
to advice
to lie to people

But words have I not used
to humiliate people
worsen pitiable conditions
but words i have not used
to murder any

Words, Words,
Words, Words

They are like
the daylight
and darkness
they can bring
life and death

For when words are use
The result is either
Positive or negative
Positive, that`s welcoming
Negative, aren't so welcoming
Thus, we should endeavor to
Use them wisely so our
consciences will serve us right

01/14
Monrovia, Liberia,

Our Sisters, Our Future

My beautiful daughters
like their male counterparts,
deserve a good life
A life free of
insecurity, suppression,
and forceful marriage
A Life of
good education, gender equity,
and happiness

All of our innocent babies
deserve a better future
But that future can only be theirs
if the world we give them offers
equal treatment in all aspects

**10/14
Monrovia, Liberia**

A Newly Wedded Sister
Tribute to Amy Soumaoro

Saturday starts a new journey for a sister
A journey full of love yet sometimes sadness
A journey of experiencing
a true womanhood
A journey that seeks to produce offspring
Such is the journey a beautiful sister
 has embarked upon
Such is the road a princess has decided to rid on
A road that can only be ridden on
By a vow of togetherness until eternity
A road that can only be ridden on based
On love, trust and understanding
"Lucky Bangalee", hold my princess as if
She was the last raw egg in this world
Like the hen would guide her chick
Guide my princess until eternity
Until the end of ages
Happy and successful journey
I wish the newly wedded couple

01/14
Monrovia, Liberia

Forgiveness

It is difficult letting go of some things.
Especially when they hurt so much
causing our tears roll down our cheeks
like a river meanders its way into the sea

It is difficult forgiving someone
who ransacked our lives and
deprived us of our happiness,
leaving us forever shattered.

Instead, we often seek revenge
We seek a way to even the score
This is only human at those times
But think for a moment, when has
revenge ever brought absolution?
What peace of mind do we obtain
through revenge?
Hmm! What satisfaction does revenge
brings us?

Isn't forgiveness, an abandoned word,
a better option in these cases?

It is very hard to let go something
Especially when it cuts too deep
It is very hard to forgive someone
who ransacked our lives

however, revenge is not and
will not be a lasting solution
it brings momentary peace

Laughter, revenge will not bring us
Peace, revenge will not bring us
Only more tears and oft regret
Like a light in darkness, so forgiveness is
It gives us the peace of mind
That the hatred had occupied
It motivates us to put our lives
Back together and move on
It allows God to push us up and
Forgive us for our mistakes as well

07/14
Monrovia, Liberia

Grandfather of Grandfathers

Grandfather of grandfathers Alhaj Nvaseki
you raised more than nineteen children
who are successful individuals today
Grandfather you
Worked very hard to fed them
Worked very hard to educate them
Worked very hard to cater to their needs
and provided that strong religious figure

Matchless in his religious practice
thus you trained your family to be
Such is the grandfather I`m blessed to
have
You may not be popular with the world
But you are the king in your own kingdom

Our Grandfather has
adoring extended family members
who see in him a leader and healer
Like King Solomon so is his wisdom
Like Nelson Mandela so is his love for humanity
Like a river, so his love for education flows

Even at 89 Grandfather still retains
those attributes of a gentleman
Time has been the best judge for all his hard work
Oh! The Giver of life please give the grandfather of grandfathers
All of the time to reap what he has sown

12/12
Monrovia, Liberia

Hate

Some harbor
hatred and jealousy
For other people

Some people allow
religion or tradition
to dictate how they feel

Other people use
family and friends
as reasons to hate

Why should we degrade
and humiliate others?
Why should we distrust
and revile others?

Are we all not the same?
Do we all not feel pain?
Are we all not humans?
We breathe, live and love
All the same, we are one
Hence let's kill this evil- hate

10/13/

Monrovia, Liberia

Family Is Precious

Our families are important
They care greatly for us
They often wipe our tears
When they run down our cheeks
They give us a helping hand
When we need it to survive

They love us unconditionally
They make us smile
even if we don`t want to
They get lonely when
we are not around
They are who anxious
to welcome us home
After a horrific experience
They offer us the needed care

Families can be awesome
At times they are awful
Like the colors of the rainbow
we learn to take the shades of
difference build relationships
For me, family is my happiness
Family is my backbone to success

06/14, Monrovia Liberia

Unity in Diversity

You are a Mano man
she is a Bassa Woman
She is a Grebo Girl
I am a Mandingo boy
That`s who we are, be proud of it

You are a Caucasian
She is a Mongolian
I am a Negro
That`s how we were born, respect it

You are a Christian
He is a Buddhist
She is a Jews
I am a Muslim
That`s how we chose to serve God, do not despise us

You are a Democrat/Republican
He is an ANC partisan
She is a CDcian or Up partisans
I am an independent
That`s our political beliefs, respect our decisions

You want to be an engineer
He wants to be a Doctor
She wants to be a politician
I want to be a public administrator
That`s our passion, stop the discouragement

You are wealthy
He is a middle class
I am a peasant
That`s our status in life
Give us the same respect

Let our diversities shine like the sun
And our unity grows deep like the river
For unity in diversity
Is the key to peaceful co-existence

01/14
Monrovia, Liberia

Our Future Today

Our world today builds
the future tomorrow
The way we live today
will influence the way
the next generation lives

The decisions we make today
The way we treat each other
The opportunities we create…

Everything we do today
Impacts the future
Hence we must be mindful
of our today's actions on tomorrow

So what are we doing?
Are we leaving the world`s
problems unsolved?
Are we creating opportunities
For the world`s poorest children?

Are we enriching the rich ones
Do we care only for ourselves?
Or are we global ambassadors
to alleviate the world`s problems?

Do we silently do nothing
Do we act on something?
When asked about our legacy
What will we say?
What answer will we give?

Are we lessening
Our children's tasks
Or multiplying them?
Oh! What are we doing today?
Oh! What are we doing today?

We must all contribute
To solving the world`s problems
For a better world today
means a better tomorrow

05/14 /Monrovia, Liberia
0

She Is Special To Me

I am really in love with her
But she loves someone else
I had started to feel that she was mine
She was about to give me a chance
But her ex was fast to re-light his torch
Of past memory and happy times
She swallowed my feelings when she
Accepted her ex`s proposal excitedly.

What can I do but accept her decision
Though my feelings for her is not declining
What can I do but accept her decision
Though she won a special place in my heart
What can I do but accept her decision
Though I never tire of her long sparkling natural hair
What can I do but accept her decision
Though it is very hard to do

03/2015/Monrovia, Liberia

Passion

Passion can make anything happen
The toughest thing can be made possible
When passion dominates its realization

Education is about passion
Work is about passion
Life is about passion

Passion must wholly dominate
Everything we set out to do
Without passion,
commitment is lacking
Without passion,
personal sacrifices cease to exist
Without passion,
everything we do is but fleeting
Without passion,
we cease to exist

08/14
Monrovia, Liberia

Underestimation

Underestimation, a not so good thing
The potentials are seen yet selfishness
Characterizes the potential's cultivation
Some just do not want to help you
Because you will be more successful than they are
Some just do not want to help you out of jealousies
Some just do not want to hear anything great about you
And others are just naturally wicked
But those who underestimate people
Only refused to accept the fact that the world is too small
Your worker today may be your boss tomorrow
Someone who you despise today
May be the one who you will need the most tomorrow

Someone who you deny
an opportunity today
May be the key to the opportunity
you will need the most
Knowing all these, you still
underestimate and humiliate people
Knowing all these you still
remain adamant for you think
Opportunity will be at your feet forever
Yet you forget to know that
opportunity is a guess
Today it visits you
Tomorrow it may be me
So utilize your guess to build potentials
Before it is too late

11/12
Monrovia, Liberia

From a Child to an Adult

Amazing how
humans develop
from our birth
through our growth
it is baffling

A child is so tiny,
innocent and beautiful
it is unaware of the
beauty or evil around
it knows not the
countless challenges
nor does it know the
many opportunities

life is amazing at all
its stages.
It is profound on
Every level
Hence we must
Value it,
Appreciate it
Respect it
Keep it... alive

09/14 /Monrovia, Liberia

You are a Damn Racist

We have different skin tone
So you are better than me?
You`re no better than me
You are just a damn racist

You calling me all sort of names
Simply to satisfy your ego
Don`t make you any better
It just means that you are a damn racist

Nothing you could possibly say
Could make me feel inferior
No amount of rejection
can distract my attention

For what matters is not whether
I am a victim of your act of racism
But it is whether I can be
That resourceful person I wish to be
That you can run to no matter the color of
my skin

11/14
Monrovia, Liberia

The World Must Wake Up

The World must wake up
Wake up to the reality that
The execution of innocent
The murder of civilians
Regardless of where they live
is unjustifiable

The world must wake up
Wake up to the reality that
the recruitment of children
as child soldiers and terrorists
is wicked

The world must wake up
Wake up to the reality
that depriving children
Access to education
is self-defeating

The world must wake up
Wake up to the reality that
climate change is a fact
We must do something
to save the future

Wake up!
Wake up!
Wake up!

Mrs. Universe
The world must wake up
and join hands together
To leave the next generation
a better world
Before it becomes too late

10/14/
Monrovia, Liberia

Sleep Oh! Sleep

Sleep Oh! Sleep
I need you but you flee
I really want to rest
Yet you abandoned me

Sleep Oh! Sleep
I`m knocking on your door
Yet I can`t get any response
I need you to come to my rescue
For I anxiously want to sleep

Sleep Oh! Sleep
I have money
Can it buy you?
I have persuasive tongue
Can you be persuaded?
What else then?
Sleep Oh! Sleep
I need you like never before

05/14
Monrovia, Liberia

Book of Poetry

I picture so much
through her words
I mentally travel
to many places
through her description
I've gone places that my
feet have never step
Yet my mind did see
Places that my eyes
have never seen
Yet my mind could envisage
They took me to places that I have never
been before

**06/14
Monrovia, Liberia**

The Rain

The rain sings me a song
that goes with a unified
and intertwine beat
A beat that within me
awakens a special feeling
sometimes indescribable
OR
but often a feeling of loveliness
and at other times, serenity
The rain sings me a song
A song that I always like to hear
For it gives me that peace of mind
A certain and relaxation
Even if I have not had one for a long time

06/14
Monrovia, Liberia

The Sky

Looking at the sky
Only leads me to imagination
Imagination that takes me to
as far as its creator
For words are inadequate to describe
The sky in all its majesty
Looking up to the sky
have often resulted
In thoughts of how it was created
And those imaginations
Have given me further reasons
To believe that the sky`s creator
Is surely the Almighty and the Most High

**08/14
Monrovia, Liberia**

They say, We ask

They said our constitution needs amendment
So they need our suggestions
They said we should go to Grand Bassa County
So they can have consultations with us
They said we are the youth leaders
From the fifteen counties
So we should represent our people at the consultation
They said we are the future
leaders of our land
So our inputs are very important
To the revision of our laws
Like a river meanders its way into the sea

So we made our way to Grand Bassa County
To answer to our generational duty

They said our constitution needs to be amended
So they need our suggestions
Then we ask:
Will political and economic interests dominate
the amendment of our laws
or will our patriotic suggestions dominate
the revision of the constitution of our nation,
Mama Liberia

7/14
Monrovia, Liberia

Why Denounced Your Culture?

Why have you denounced your culture?
Why have you underrated your culture?
Is it because you went across the sea?
Is that why you act pompous to your own?
Or you tasted the Whiteman's culture?
Or ride his trains or airplanes that take you
long distances with less pain?

Why have you denounced your culture?
Have you eaten the Whiteman's raw
leaves that you consider the sweetest?
Have you taken your shower in his
swimming pool or pipe borne water that
you consider pure?
Answer me, why have you denounced
your own culture so much that you hate
to speak your dialects;
so much that you hate everything African
and embrace everything western
so much that you rarely identify with your
own family

Why have you denounced your own culture?
Don`t you know that the African culture nurture your great Ancestors
Why have you denounced your own culture?
Will the white man accept you in his culture?
Will you be a caricature of his culture forever?
Will you pay the price for a culture free person?
Regardless, the African culture will continue to exist
Whether you stay or not, the African culture will continue to be cherished
Like the sun, so the African culture
Will continue to shine until the end of age

02/13
Monrovia, Liberia

I smell World War III

I smell World War III
though I don`t pray for it
The international stage is blazing like fire
Power alliances and
allies over protection flourish
The remote causes of World War I and II
Are gradually resurfacing
Peace is regularly being undermined
While war is slowly being held in high
regard

I smell World War III, though I am hopeful
that
Dialogue will triumph over violence
I smell World War III, though I am hopeful
that
Peace will ultimately win over every other
thing.

03/13
Monrovia, Liberia

Liberia Never Bows Down

What haven't you withstood
Mama Liberia?
The struggle for Independence
wounded you
still you conquered
The marginalization of the 80s
ransacked you
still you conquered
The Coup d'état put you on 'last legs'
still you conquered
The 1990` massacres tore you apart
still you conquered
The 2000 bloodshed wiped you aware
still you conquered
Ebola nearly buried you
still you conquered
The present challenges
vow despair and cynicism
still you will conquer
For what have you not withstood
Mama Liberia?
The Liberia I know conquers
foes and trials of any difficulty
Even at 169, Mama Liberia never bows
For what have you not withstood
Dear Mama Liberia?

Poverty

Their bellies swell from hunger
I wonder how they feel
Imagine what they are undergoing
The pain must be unbearable
And their hopes all gone
like the wind, they are directionless

Sadly, our world has abandoned them
Like they do not exist
Barely do they get a good meal
Talk less of securing a better future
I tear up at such a condition
Not just because our world is cruel to them
But because poverty has swollen them
Poverty has ransacked their lives
Yet we do nothing for them

01/15
Monrovia, Liberia

Friends

Friends!
Some are wonderful others are not
Some elevate themselves to family
While others diminish into enemies

Friends!
Some make us smile others make us cry
Some care about us even more than
family; while some feign love but destroy us

Friends!
We need them at one time or another
Some are buddies that may know us well
But choose to be mute
Some know a little but spread rumors
Some are assets others are but burdens

Friends!
No matter what, we often seek advice
From them at some point in time
But never should we place absolute
Confidence in them at all times

03/13
Monrovia, Liberia

Family is Everything

Family is everything
The light in darkness
The nail that hooks the line
when the rope cuts
The hope when everything is lost
The smiles when tears fill a barrel
The calm when temper is hot

Family is absolutely everything
What is a man without family
The fabrics of success
What is this life without family
The backbone of our existence
What are we without families?
The people who stay with us
In every situation

What are we then without family?
Our sincere but unpaid advisors
Hmm! Family is absolutely everything
And that`s why the day
We are disconnected from them
Our world turns upside down
For family is everything
Including the very air we breathe

06/14
Monrovia, Liberia

My Mother, My Best Friend

Happy Mother's day my best friend
Just as I'm oblige as a Muslim
to pray everyday
So it is my duty to love and care for you
Like gold, so my love glitters for you
Even if threatened with placing
the sun in my left hand
And the moon in my right hand
to stop loving you, I will never stop

For how can I stop loving
the air I breath
The strength I use to do things
The brain I use to study
And the food I eat to keep me healthy
As a fish dies upon leaving water
Likewise the day I stop loving you
My time on this earth will be over
Happy Mother's day Mommy

Mother`s Day/14
Monrovia, Liberia

Priceless Gift

Children are the greatest
gift from God
Mothers soon forget
the 9 months of pain
when their beautiful faces appear
Children bring happiness and love
For some, they can bring hope and strength
in matrimonial relationships

For others, such relationships are
incomplete without these angels
Children are future heroes
to their parents
Although some fail
in realizing this dream
they still carry lingering hopes

But let's remember that children are our future
And their future depends on the values we teach them
For these values will give them courage to stand tall
Even in the face of life's greatest challenges
For these values will require blending love and discipline
Like shadows so our children are a replica of who we are
So let's teach and show them the awesome qualities that they should possess
For these beautiful angels deserve to be happy
No matter where they are

09/14
Monrovia, Liberia

Replica of the Devil's home

All of the Global Media Outlets
Are reporting death news and tragedies
Switching to CNN, only news of
Plane crashes I am greeted with
BBC is about kidnappings and so...
Maybe Aljazeera will be okay, thought I
But Aljazeera is about the murdering
Of innocent people by a suicide bomber
And Africa 24 is about Ebola and poverty
Oh! What a world we are living in?
A world where death, hunger and sicknesses
Are news reported every minute
Will a day ever pass without hearing about tragedies?
Hmm! I don't know what's next
But all I know is that our present world
Is a replica of the devil's home

07/14
Monrovia, Liberia

We have heard about their coming

We have heard about their coming
So we are anxiously awaiting them
Our people are dying and
our situation is deteriorating
Our worries are increasing and
the tears are uncountable

We have heard about the
sending of US marines
And we can`t wait to see them on our soil
Helping to put our conflict under control
Oh! Many tears have already been shed
Oh! Many lives have already been lost
Oh! Many Children have been made
orphans
Oh! Poverty is exacerbating our conditions
We can`t bear it anymore
So the news of their coming is
the most talk about in town
Like fish needs water,
so we need their intervention now
For they are now the light in darkness to us
In this time of Ebola

10/14
Monrovia, Liberia

My High School Secret Admirer

Dear high school secret admirer
I really do miss you and I don`t know
how life is treating you
I have not even seen you since we bided
farewell to high school
I can`t really stop imagining your soft smile
And the sweat sound of your voice

Dear my high school secret admirer
I really do miss seeing your beautiful face
 The last time I saw it was during our
graduation
When we took some lovely pictures
How long can I wait to see your lovely
smiles again!

Dear my high school secret admirer
I really do miss walking down the steps
alongside you
With my rough palm in your soft one
Just for you, I will choose to spend another
ten months
In school to see your face everyday
That`s how much I really do miss you

Dear high school secret admirer
I contacted you via phone, but to no avail
I walked long distances just to see you, but to no avail
I tried to get you out of my head, but to no avail
Flipping through our lovely high school pictures, is
Is it my high school secret admirer?
Or my secret admirer even beyond high school
Hmm! I really do hope you will understand how much
I really do miss you and everything about you and our time in high school
And it seems like you are still my secret admirer even beyond

09/14
Monrovia, Liberia

Motivation

Motivation keeps me
when I think it`s over
When I am like: hmm!
I can`t make it
it renews my commitment
it makes me to carry on

it tells me to:
keep working hard
that I can make it

it makes me to
face the storm
keep my head up

And focus when things get rocky
Wow! Motivation, motivation, motivation
It is so powerful to me that
I prefer it to luxuries

First Love Experience

Experiencing intimate love
for the first time was amazing
How tenderly she treated me
and I reciprocated it
How dumbfounded I was hearing
Her sweet voice calling me "Darling"
How generous it was to surprise me
With petty but lovely gifts
Her visitations were characterized
By laughter, jokes and lovely things
We never thought of sex. To us,
it seemed a distraction from our dreams

Experiencing intimate love
for the first time was funny
How funny it sounded hearing someone
Attach "Darling or Sweetie" to my name
How funny it was looking at each other
And smiling without saying anything
Her jokes made me laugh so much
That she would beg me to stop
I woke each morning to her text messages
Wow! It was wonderful being in love for the
first time and such an experience will
remain with me forever.

My Africa, Your Africa, Our Africa

My Africa, Your Africa, Our Africa
My Africa of pride and generosity
Your Africa of charity
Our Africa of vast natural resources

My Africa of ancestry and bonhomie
Your Africa of poverty and disease
Our Africa of dependency

My Africa, Your Africa, Our Africa
My Africa of friendly people and ideal culture
Your Africa of inferiority and corruption
Our Africa of investment

My Africa of innovative youth
My Africa of energetic youth
Your Africa of incapacitated youth
Our Africa of population growth

My Africa, Your Africa, Our Africa
My Africa will always be the way
I see my sweet land to be
Your Africa will always be your
Perception or research about my dear continent

Our Africa will always be
our common beliefs
Like the certainty of tides
So I will continue to cherish
no matter what
My dear Africa

08/12
Monrovia, Liberia

We are tired with you Mr. President

Our people are tired with you
They don`t want you at the top
They don't want you anymore
They don`t want you piloting
the plane anymore
We are tired with you

Our people are tired with you
How do you want them to express it?
For they have voted you out
but you refused to go
By rigging elections
By changing constitutions
We are tired with you

Our people are tired with you
Cracking down on dissent is not the answer
Imprisoning opposition will not help
When the people are tired with you
They are surely tired with you
Nothing changes that we're tired with you

Our people are tired with you
Why don`t you peacefully go
Resulting to war out of selfishness

Will only terrorize our people
Will only exacerbate poverty
Will only make the bright future
we dream of vaguer. We're tired

Our people are tired with you
Are fifteen years or more captaining
the ship not enough for you?
What have you even done with the time?
Leave because the people say you should
Go Mr. President, we want a different
driver at the top. We are tired with you

Our people are tired with you
You have failed us
You have stolen from us
You denied us so much for so long
Our people don't want you
Anymore. Go Mr. President
We survived as a country
without you. Go Mr. President
We will also survive and
do even better without you
We are tired with you

01/15
Monrovia, Liberia

Liberia's Future

Have you ever wonder
about Liberia's future?
Can you show me the future
custodians of our natural resources?
Does Liberia even have a bright future?
Who will give Liberia that better future?
Did I heard you say the young people
You mean the young people who have
made nightclubs their second homes?
Or the young ones glued to their books?
Do you mean those of the attia shops?
Or the ones with practical solutions?
I'm really confused, please tell me

Is it the young people with integrity?
Or the young people lacking integrity?
Is it the young people of Miami Beach?
Like a scholar, is inquisitive I wish to know

Which young people
do you refer to?
I really wish to know
Do you refer to the young people
who fake documents to get employ?
Or the young people who study overtime
thus eventually landing the good jobs?
Is it the young people who
dream of a better Liberia?
Or the young people who
see Liberia as elephant meat?
Night after night,
I wonder about Liberia`s future
For I wish to see Liberia`s future
leaders
Then I will predict Liberia`s future

01/14
Monrovia, Liberia

Bye Bye Ebola

It has been sixteen months of trials
Our enemy has finally let go of us
And our country is free from her grips
Free from the Enemy,
Free from the Enemy

It has been sixteen months of tribulations
Months of pain as we watched
our compatriots die like ants
our country come to a standstill
Months that we will never forget

For in those months
life was hell for many of us
there was no safe haven
from a hidden enemy

Now that the enemy
has finally let go of us
how do we ensure
that it doesn't comeback?

A moment of meditation
and prayers we must all make
But importantly,
we must never forget
our experiences and lives lost
While we rejoice for our freedom

We must retain the safety and
anti Ebola measures that saved us
we should make them part of our customs

We must also pray for our neighbors
For until they can be free from
the enemy, we are still at risk

It has been sixteen months of trials
But finally, the enemy has let go of us
Your visitation was painstaking
Please con't visit us again Ebola
Bye Bye Ebola, Bye Bye Ebola

05/15
Monrovia, Liberia

Rest in Peace Big Dad Ansumana

Few days ago, you sent me
on an errand along with mawa
your voice sounded so strong
and impressive as always
Days after, you are no more

Your death news is something
I can`t easily accept
For a father and inspiration you were to me
Despite the distance between us
you never stopped motivating me
to always value education
You were my primary link to
My paternal family members
You took me to 'Wolodu Soqua'
family meetings

It really pains me knowing that
You have left us; left at a time when
the guidance you gave is yielding
Tears is what I am full of
For you are irreplaceable to us
Rest in peace. Forever we will miss you

02/14
Monrovia, Liberia

Africa Needs You Back

You have gone to the West
To satisfy your thirst for knowledge
Now that you have acquired the
Bachelors, Masters, and PhDs
Your continent needs you back
to build the capacity of our people
Return, not to join the corrupted
but to enhance accountability
Return to improve transparency
not to deepen on the scarcity
Return to innovate, to help, to do;
not to increase the unemployment rate
Return to create more jobs

Africa needs you back
Will you answer our dear continent`s call?
Or will you refuse to give back to Africa?
Hmmm! Whatever the case is
The ball is in your court
Africa needs your knowledge
Africa needs you to educate; to empower
her rapidly growing youthful population

10/2014
Monrovia, Liberia

Soweto Oh! Soweto

There you were yesteryears
Struggling young students
were gunned down
In cold blood
Because they stood up

Soweto Oh! Soweto
This day rewinds our memories
The flashback of blood
and massacre
Clouds our imagination
Even as we write today

Soweto Oh! Soweto
That day was bloody
Its remembrance is fresh
Sowetan students I see
Hector Pieterson I picture
Bloody peasant children
Gunned down.... Oh Soweto!

Soweto Oh! Soweto
You we celebrate on this day
Education for the African Child
We cherish on this day
Many 'Orlando West High School'
We yearn for on this day

Soweto Oh! Soweto
Your memory cripples my day
Yet renews my hope for tomorrow
Breathtakingly you've moved on
But all is not well with the African Child

Soweto Oh! Soweto
Sleep in Peace Sowetans
For your memory still inflames
Our quest for
A better education and livelihood
For the African Child

How dey you

How dey you kill innocence
in the name of Islam
Which portion of the Koran
told you so?
How dey you turn kids
into suicide bombers
in the name of Islam
Which portion of the Koran
told you so?
How dey you bully and
rape women
in the name of Islam
Which portion of the Koran
told you so?
How dey you suppress,
dehumanize and capture
people of other religion
in the name of Islam.
Which portion of the Koran
told you so?

How dey you?
How dey you?

Why defame our
peaceful Religion?
Why make it out
as a violent one?
Why stigmatize
our humble women
by showing such
religious disrespect?
Why make us out
to be hateful women
Why degrade our
peaceful Religion
Why defame our Islam?
Oh! You will never succeed in your
diabolical actions
In the name of our Religion, Islam

06/14 Monrovia, Liberia

ABOUT THE AUTHOR

Mohammed Donzo is an emerging voice on the Liberian literary scene. His passion for poetry goes back to his high school days when he often found himself writing poetry. He nursed this desire until it blossomed into the book you re now reading, Our Future. The selection of poems in Our Future comes from a larger collection he wrote over many years.

Mohammed is an international member of Amnesty International and facilitated the Amnesty International "Write for Rights Campaign 2014" in Liberia.

Amongst the many activists around the world, he was selected for an interview because despite the Ebola Outbreak in his country, the program was executed successfully.

He is a student of Public Administration at the University of Liberia and has undergone several online training courses from the University of

Macquarie in Australia, and the Western Sydney University through the Open 2 Study Australia platform.

The author has also been active in local and national youth advocacy since secondary school days.

Currently, he is the Executive Director and Co-Founder of Prepare Africa Incorporated - PAI, a pan African organization concentrated on raising awareness about elections and good governance in Africa. Along with the amazing team of PAI from other African countries, they recently launched the youth magazine, *Africa Moment Magazine.*

COMING SOON!

The Answer of Patriots – The story of how patriotism conquered fear and danger during the Ebola Outbreaks in Liberia.

    The author played a significant role in the fight against Ebola. He led pro-bono community awareness at the height of the Ebola Outbreaks, work with the Coalition of Organizations Against Ebola pro-bono to mobilize community organizations in the fight against Ebola, work with the Elections Commission as Voters Identification Officer during the heated Senatorial Elections in the midst of Ebola, raised massive awareness about the Reopening of Schools and students' preparedness during the Ebola Outbreaks amongst others.

    Watch out for this Memoir detailing his experiences in the field and with community organizations and why he risk his life to help his country beat the scourge of Ebola.

www.ingramcontent.com/pod-product-compliance
Lightning Source LLC
Chambersburg PA
CBHW071201090426
42736CB00012B/2412